Help! My Child is Starting Middle School!

Sugar

Flour 2/3

mix

1/3 sugar

3 egs
gonna use 2

beat it

oil 2tsp

Help! My Child is Starting Middle School!

A Survival Handbook for Parents

What Parents and Students Should Know the
First Year of Middle School

Jerry L. Parks, Ed.S., NBCT
Georgetown Middle School
Georgetown, KY

Weekly Reader Press
New York Lincoln Shanghai

Help! My Child is Starting Middle School!
A Survival Handbook for Parents

Weekly Reader Press
an imprint of iUniverse, Inc.
and the Weekly Reader Corporation

iUniverse books may be ordered through booksellers or by contacting:

iUniverse
2021 Pine Lake Road, Suite 100
Lincoln, NE 68512
www.iuniverse.com
1-800-Authors (1-800-288-4677)

Because of the dynamic nature of the Internet, any Web addresses or links contained in this book may have changed since publication and may no longer be valid.

The views expressed in this work are solely those of the author and do not necessarily reflect the views of the publisher, and the publisher hereby disclaims any responsibility for them.

ISBN: 978-0-595-46529-3

Printed in the United States of America

Contents

Author acknowledgements

I would like to offer a special thanks to all the parents and students at Georgetown Middle School for making this book possible.

I would also like to thank Sharan Gwynn and Vicky Grant, colleagues of mine at school, for their help in the writing and editing of this book.

Finally, I would like to express appreciation to my principals, Tommy Hurt and Jim Masters, for all the support they have given me as a teacher, and Dr. Dallas Blankenship, Superintendent of the Scott County Schools, for his camaraderie and friendship over the last fifteen years.

What is a Middle Schooler?

A middle schooler is random motion, jumbled chaos, and predictable unpredictability—a child becoming an adult—paused for one magical moment between pictures of puppies, and pin-ups of sex symbols. They are a walking paradox of fashionless style, fueled by hormones and gum, and fired by engines that seem to never run out of gas. They are strongly independent social creatures that travel in packs, and communicate by sacred note. They are nourished by the immediate, unencumbered by past, and impatient for the tomorrow they feel will never come.

Middle schoolers can miss the obvious, harp on the obscure, and defend the impossible. They thrive on spontaneity, loathe predictability, and refuse to even acknowledge the parents they love. They deny the proven, dispute the certain, stand up for the irrelevant, and fall out of chairs. Tapping is their anthem, and fairness—their rule of life. They are possessed of selective memory, and a fierce loyalty to their own kind. Their hair is their banner, disorder—their creed. Their image is the only thing that matters more than lunch.

Middle schoolers are bolts of energy wrapped in a package of laziness. They are confusion poured into mood swings—fueled by encouragement, motivated by curiosity, and stimulated by challenge. They are inspired by sincerity, frustrated by denial, and defeated by doubt. They are gangly growth spurts with a twinkle in their eyes. They are confident pretenders masquerading in fragile shells of insecurity—trusting skeptics—secretly searching for heroes.

Middle schoolers love to be hugged, but hate to be touched. They are reactive agents who cling to routine while reaching for change. They are reminders of our own immortality; in-progress paradigms of possibility in whose lives we plant a lesson, shape a behavior, mold a character and seal a destiny. They are the first blooms of tomorrow's hope—fleeting sunbeams of a thirteenth springtime—on loan to a winter world.

J. Parks

Excerpted *from "Teacher Under Construction"*
© Weekly Reader Press, iUniverse Publishers

Preface

"Teaching carries with it the unstated assumption that the student has a problem, and the teacher always has the answer."

This book was written to help parents and their middle schoolers successfully integrate into the wonderful world of middle school. Middle schoolers are like no one else. They are not little adults; neither are they taller primary schoolers. Teaching middle school is the most difficult teaching assignment of all. It is also the most rewarding.

Parents are seldom—if ever—prepared for the enormous changes their child faces entering middle school. The sheltered, structured, and nurturing environment that is elementary school gives way to the fast-paced, organized chaos of middle school. Students often feel more *thrown* into, rather than *eased* into, the middle school world, and parents of first-time middle schoolers often feel more lost than their children. The sixth grade is the time when Mom and Dad start to feel they are losing their little one forever, and—in a very real sense—they are.

Nothing in this book presents concepts that are new or profound, and no individual can presume to know perfectly the mind of a middle schooler. *"Help! My Child is Starting Middle School!"* is merely an effort to help parents and their children get off to a successful start in middle school. Chapters 4, 5 & 6 are the most important chapters in the book, and this book is designed to be read from general overview principles to instructions that are more specific. That's how chapters are arranged. It's also how middle schoolers learn.

Although primarily written for parents, portions of the book can be read and used by middle schoolers themselves. At the end of each chapter is a section entitled *"How will you handle this?"* Here, are presented numerous real-world middle school situations which may very well occur. As these are read, parents should consider how they might address the situations, and then discuss with their child their thoughts, and how they might deal with alternatives. In discussing these together, both parent and middle schooler will be better prepared for what's coming in middle school. At the end of the book is an

Appendix, with what is hoped are some helpful materials for parent and child to utilize together.

To glean the best from the book, below is the author's recommendation.

1. Parents, read the book through alone first.

2. Allow the middle schooler to read chapter 2, and discuss the chapter with them.

3. Read and discuss with the middle schooler chapters 3-8 over the course of week or so.

4. Reread chapters 2-8 with the middle schooler, specifically discussing the *How would you handle this?* examples in the chapters.

1. Dear Mom and Dad: *Your child and their school—the uniqueness they bring, and the least you need to know*

Dear Mom and Dad

Parents: You have now arrived at the point where your voice begins to no longer be the most important voice in your child's life.

Giving up your son or daughter to middle school is traumatic. You have nurtured them for the last eleven years, and you're in no hurry to surrender their childhood. But, to some degree—as they begin middle school—you must let them go. Up to this point, you, and what you say, have been among the most important aspects of your child's life. From this point on, their own developing interests—and the opinions of their peers—will become their primary influences. Middle school is the time to let them stretch their wings.

Letting them stretch their wings, however, does not mean giving up your involvement in their lives. In fact, as middle schoolers, they will need your support more than ever. As they try to balance the activities and responsibilities of middle school life (and you will have to help them), you must make them understand that schoolwork is *Job One.*

Middle schoolers develop in ways in which they will never develop again. Sixth grade is a time of great change in the adolescent brain. This is the year children become better able to move from the concrete thoughts into the abstract world of theory and possibility. They learn *empathy,* not just sympathy, and their concept of the world grows by leaps and bounds. Children become able to think of the world, issues, and concepts in a more global perspective. They begin to understand that there is more to living in the world than they have encountered to this point in their lives, and that other people's realities are different from theirs, and will influence the way they think and act.

Brain development in seventh graders causes them to develop further independence and self-expression. Irrationality and emotional upheaval can cause them to no longer be the child you remember. They reach for anything

1

and grab for everything. Seventh graders begin to settle into the new realities they discovered in the sixth grade. Eighth grade, while a somewhat less chaotic period, is a time of strengthening relationships, and a time when what *you* say begins to have an even lessening impact. By this point, your child is no longer a child, and is rapidly becoming what they are going to grow up to be.

Middle schoolers' brains actually map new ways of thinking and grow in capacity. This is the time period of rapid growth in the physical and mental worlds of your child. Because of this, they may not always think logically, or even clearly, but they're doing the best they can. Your job is to help them get through this time, and keep them grounded in the morality you taught them their first eleven years, so they can grow and become the best people they can possibly be.

Mom and Dad—you are your child's first teachers. All teachers which follow you in the teaching of your child must build upon the foundation you have already laid. While middle school teachers are not, and do not try to be, parents to your child, it is extremely important for your child to develop a positive relationship with adults at school. Understanding that, there are some things at home that you would do well to remember in order to help facilitate this process.

1. *Be prepared for change.* The middle school years are a time of change and turmoil—in your child's life and in yours. Middle schoolers' physical and emotional changes will abound too. So will what they learn—academically and non-academically—at school. Be prepared for the shock of personal and school discussions on topics you never heard your child mention while they were in elementary school. Don't avoid these discussions. Address them with your child. Middle school is a whole new world. Unfortunately, it is not the *ideal* world you wish it could be. It is the real world of kids being kids, where not everyone your child meets will be a role model. Be open in your discussions with your kids, and understand that you cannot solve all their problems. Neither can you win all the 'wars'. Choose your battles. Accept the fact that your middle schooler is moving in a direction that might not seem to be precisely the one you planned for them. Guide them and trust them. Allow them to develop.

2. *Teachers are allies*—not enemies—in teaching your child to be the best middle schooler they can be. While every teacher is different, please do not view your child's teacher as an *adversary*. On the other hand, remember, the teacher's job is first to *protect* your child, second to *teach* them, and only third, to *like* them. Whether you want to hear it or not, your child's teachers will never love them they way you do. Get to know the teachers, keep in contact, and understand—regardless of what your child comes home and tells you—there is always, *always*—another side to the story. See your child's teachers as co-workers, not adversaries. However, just to be on the safe side, remind your middle schooler that if any teacher should ever say: *"don't tell your parents"*, that's a red flag for your child to come home and do just that.

3. *Teachers are not peers of your child.* Do not see them as such. As there is no actual 'equal rights' at home between you and your child, neither is there an 'equality' between middle schoolers and their teachers. Teachers, like parents, are the adults here, and in reality, middle schoolers generally appreciate and accept that relationship. Remind your child that they do not talk back to their teachers, and that you will not tolerate negative conversation about teachers at home.

4. *Ask your child to teach you at least three new things they learned each day!* Listening is one of the greatest—and most neglected—skills of parenting. Discuss daily school activities each evening. Don't be too busy with the little stuff in life to miss the important moments with your child. When they tell you about their day, look them in the eye, and listen; *really* listen! Middle schoolers know when you care, and really care that you want to know.

5. *Get involved.* Research has shown that parent participation increases the child's self-esteem, improves their academic performance, improves the parent-child relationship, and develops a more positive attitude toward school in both the parent and child. Get involved in your child's middle school life. Plan at least one visit to *each* of your child's classes during the year, and attend school functions as often as you are able. While it certainly is not always possible, as a general rule: parents who *care* are parents who're *there*.

6. **Be tolerant** of a low score every once and awhile, but never, *never* accept a 'zero' without finding out why. All middle schoolers have off days, but a zero is either a careless *attitude* or a lesson unlearned, and both are disastrous to academic performance and character development. Do not let a zero slide. Not even one. (See Chapter 3)

7. **Don't encourage calling home.** Middle schoolers need strict parental rules regarding the use of cell phones, as well as calling home in general. Emergencies are one thing. But forgotten homework, changes of clothing, etc., are seldom reasons to call home. Teach your child to be responsible. Do not cater to the desire to call home for non-emergencies. It is a nuisance to teachers and disruptive to the learning environment.

8. **Reward positive accomplishments** (agenda book completely filled in, perfect papers, etc.) on a *weekly* basis. An ounce of positive feedback is worth more than a pound of criticism. (Unfortunately, it won't be remembered nearly as long.) A little goes a long way, and middle schoolers thrive on praise. Really make a big deal about successes. It matters to your middle schooler now. As they grow older, it will matter less and less.

9. **Be a parent—not a friend.** Lay down firm rules and consequences at home, and hold your child *accountable* (see Chapter 7). When they bring you pleading excuses, don't get sucked into their drama. They don't need you to be their friend—they have plenty of those. They need you to *take authority* and direct them. That's what children lack. Say this three times: *"They need me to be their parent, not their buddy!"* Your middle schooler feels more secure when you correct them than when you indulge them. Correction is *positive,* not a negative. They'll complain at first, appreciate it eventually, and thank you for the rest of their lives. Remember—even though you can't be a perfect parent, you can still be a *good* one. Care enough to discipline, and to say *no.*

10. **Be objective.** Listen to your child's teachers. Sometimes they may tell you things about your child you aren't going to like or want to hear. But remember, your child at home is not necessarily the same child they see at school. There may be problems you haven't been shown

yet at home. Teachers also offer fresh eyes to behaviors you may have gotten used to. You don't have to take everything the teacher says as gospel, but make sure you really *listen* and consider their advice. They are in this profession because they *care*. Not for the dough.

Here are some further brief, but important things for you to remember. Most are discussed elsewhere in the book.

The Ten Commandments for Parents

1. Check your child's agenda book *daily,* and check not only homework, but *completed* homework on a regular basis. Do it! (This cannot be overemphasized.)

2. Keep lines of communication with school open. Don't wait for school to contact you. Take the initiative.

3. Do not assume your child is always telling the whole story.

4. Require a set study and homework time and place. Make it routine.

5. Understand that the teachers cannot love your child as much as you do.

6. Keep scheduled conferences and times. Value the teachers' time as much as you do yours. They have families too.

7. Tell administrators about teachers who make a positive impression. Do you enjoy being complimented? So do teachers.

8. Be *consistent* in discipline at home. Do not bluff with idle threats.

9. Never allow your child to miss school unless absolutely necessary, and schedule appointments that do not cause your child to miss the same class over and over.

10. Do not allow your child to spend an inordinate amount of time at home alone.

How will you handle this?

- o   Your child comes home and tells you the teacher refused to let them make up a missed assignment.

- o   Your child tells you they do not think it's fair that the teacher can use a cell phone in class and they can't.

- o   Your child tells you that they received a zero on an assignment they don't remember ever being given.

- o   You receive a discipline report from the teacher stating that your child was caught cheating on an exam, or copying another student's work.

- o   The school suggests that your child might need testing for a learning disorder you have never noticed.

- o   Your child tells you that your visiting one of their classes would embarrass the life out of them.

2. For Kids Only: *Welcome to middle school—This chapter is just for you!*

Dear student: *Hooray! You're coming to middle school!*

Although you don't want everybody to know it, deep down inside, you're a little bit scared, aren't you? Maybe you've had an older brother or sister already prepare you a little, but admit it—you are nervous about the new world you're about to enter! That's what this book is for—to help smooth the path from elementary to middle school! Sit down with Mom or Dad and learn how to succeed in middle school. First, let's understand a few things.

1. *Middle school counts.* Your grades will be much more important from here on than they've ever been before. Take them seriously. But more on that later. Did you know there are even scholarships (that's *money!*) you can apply for online—some as early as the 6th grade?

2. *You are unique among all the kids you will join.* You are not just someone lost in the crowd (although you might feel you are often, and wish you were sometimes!). You bring special talents and gifts that you must learn to *share* with others (see Chapter 7). Maybe you don't know exactly what those talents and gifts are right now—or maybe you do. But these will develop over the next few years. Recognize your strengths, your gifts, and your talents. Nourish them. Share them. *Don't hide them!*

3. *Friendships are going to change.* You don't want to hear this, but friendships change dramatically in middle school. I know this is a bit scary, but it's true. You will make new friendships, while you and some of your friends from elementary school will go your separate ways. Remember—you don't *own* your friends, and don't let your friends own you. Middle school is a time of great change. Choose friends wisely. You'll find you become more and more like who they are.

4. ***Don't be afraid to try new things!*** Oh yes, some 'new things' may be things you know are wrong. Of course you shouldn't try those (more on that later too). But get involved in activities that allow you to use your interests and talents. You may not be good at *everything* you try, but at least *try.* Whether it's sports, drama, dance team, academic team, or just a club—get involved. That's a big part of what middle school is all about. (But never forget—*schoolwork* is what you're there for.) Try new things! Get involved!

The keys that unlocks your success!

OK, now that we're underway, here are some other keys that will unlock your success in middle school. Mom or Dad can help you understand some of these a little better.

1. *First impressions last a long time.* We'll talk more about this later in Chapter 6. Just remember—in middle school—starting off on the right foot is more important than you may think! How you dress, how you speak, how you present yourself that first week of school— these may not change who you *are,* but it will make everyone form an opinion about you. Make sure it's a good one!

2. *Attitude is everything.* You will get frustrated. You may even get angry. But how you handle those things will be what kids and teachers are watching. Whatever you do, don't forget this: *Never whine in middle school!* Keep a positive, friendly, and cooperative attitude about things, and you will find getting along in middle school will be much easier. Even if you don't think this really works, *it does!* (More on this in Chapter 6.)

3. *Expect some big differences.* Middle school is not just a bigger elementary school. It's a different world. Yes, you will have more freedom. But also, the kids are bigger, the halls are more crowded, and everything will seem to move much faster and be less structured. You'll get used to it. Speaking of other kids, be prepared to meet and have classes with kids from many cultures and backgrounds. Some will have different learning styles than you do. They will also have different types of personalities, traditions, and even different religious backgrounds than yours. They will also feel just as (or

more) strongly about their beliefs as you do about yours, and won't appreciate ridicule. Middle school is where you learn not just about the world, but also about the *people* of the world, and how to accept differences in others without giving up the strong beliefs of your own.

4.   *Hang in there when everything seems to fall apart!* OK, this day WILL come, so get ready! The day when your locker won't open, and your schedule takes you to the wrong teacher—when your backpack spills everything in the hall, and you feel like crying, but don't dare—when your best efforts of the day feel like you're peddling through mud, and your best friend won't even speak to you—what that day comes, *hang in there!* This stuff happens to every middle schooler. But believe it or not, someday you will look back on middle school as one of the most fun times of your life. I promise.

OK kids, here are the middle school *"Twelve Commandments"*! Follow these and you will live a long (well, three years) and happy life in middle school!

1.   *I will remember the nine words that can change my life.* (Not to mention help me: get better grades, earn respect from my teachers, make more friends, and solve a million problems!):

"Yes, sir/ma'am."

"No, sir/ma'am."

"Please"

"Thank you."

"I'm sorry."

Believe it or not, learning to say these magic words will do more to help you with teachers, administrators, other students (even parents!), than just about any other words you can say. Most kids *cannot* say them. They really can't. These words just don't roll off your tongue easily! Learn to use these words *wisely* and *sincerely* and you will be treated differently by just about everyone. *These words, spoken appropriately, will make a lasting impression*—especially on your teachers. And you just might end up with better grades too. The words really will change your life in ways you don't even understand yet.

2.   *I will learn to ask for help.* Teachers can't read your mind. They don't always know when *you* don't know. When you don't understand, *ask!* Chances are, someone else has the same question. Remember—although you don't want to draw attention to yourself, you are only hurting yourself when you fail to ask questions you need answers for. Also, if you are having trouble in a class, get up your nerve and go talk to the teacher *privately*. Ask if there's a way to improve your grade. But here's a little secret: try to avoid the words *extra credit*.

3.   *I will use all methods of communication.* You will have many classes, many different assignments, and many different ways to earn grades. Keep an agenda book for these. Write things down! Write *everything* down! Do not assume you'll remember—you won't. If your teacher uses an online web page such as *Schoolnotes*, make it a habit to visit the site daily. If the teacher is willing to give it, ask for his/her email address so that you and your parents can contact them if necessary. A lack of communication is one of the biggest reasons grades go down in middle school. So is disorganization.

4.   *I will know and follow my teachers' classroom rules.* Rules, rules, rules. Not only do you have to keep *school* rules, but every *teacher* has their own list, too! Want to know a secret? Your teachers' classroom rules are very personal to them. When you violate those rules, or act as though they aren't important, it's like a personal insult. *Go with the flow.* Rules for hall passes, pencil sharpening, raising your hand—all these are important in getting along with teachers in middle school. Follow them. Act like you care. It will go a long way.

5.   *I will come to school, and be on time to class.* Tardy is one of those dirty words to middle school teachers. Being tardy as a *habit* might just get you the death penalty! Always try to be on time to your classes. If you must be late, bring a note from the previous teacher. Tardy tells the teacher their time isn't as important as yours is. Tardy is another of those personal insults middle school teachers take to

heart. It really is. It is better to have to leave a class early than to arrive at one late.

6.   *I will have, and bring, my required supplies to class.* Here's another of those things middle school teachers take personally when you don't do it. Sure, everybody forgets things once and awhile. But failing to bring the required supplies on a regular basis gives the impression you don't care about the class. You don't want to give this impression to a middle school teacher. It's like kicking their dog or something!

7.   *I will make sure my teachers know me.* Huh? Make sure my teachers know me? Isn't that what those awful seating charts are for? Teachers have a hundred or more students. You have only a handful of teachers. Here's another secret: most teachers learn the names of the kids *who make an impression* first. Yes, often that's the kids who cause trouble. But you will make a huge, *positive* impact on your teachers if you help them learn your name early in the year by doing *positive* things. You really don't want to hide in the corner in middle school. *Do something good*, even if it's being especially polite. Or, you could *really* make the teachers remember you in a positive way by never forgetting #1 above!

8.   *I will do everything in my power to stay on good terms with my teachers.* You will have to 'live' in the same building with your teachers for the next three years. Teachers are different. (Well yes, they are *different,* but that's not the point!) Some teachers and classes—you will really like. Others, not so much. One teacher may be your favorite. But don't expect all your teachers to be or act the same. Some will gladly share parts of their personal life with you. But some may not appreciate any reference to it, so watch what you ask, and don't get your feelings hurt. Allow teachers to be themselves— just like you want them to allow *you* the same privilege. Respect *all* teachers in the same way. Don't cause hurt feelings by talking about teachers you may not like as well as you do others. Teachers hear about such, and, as with students, teachers talk too. Just be respectful to all your teachers, and never give them a reason to think negatively of you. It will make the year go a whole lot smoother!

9. *I will remember The Golden Rule.* Sorry, but you're not going to get along with everybody in middle school. You have to deal with a lot of people, and in trying to get along with them, there will be some days when you may not be able to make things better, but you sure might make things worse. Remember, the world doesn't revolve around you, and others might be having a tough time as well. Try to give difficult people a break if you can, and don't judge a book by its cover, or a person by their appearance, or by just *one* impression. Treat others the way you'd *want* to be treated, not just how you think they're treating you.

10. *I will learn how to forgive.* Everyone's allowed to grow up and make mistakes! Second chances are for *everyone*, including you. Kids aren't perfect, and even teachers have bad days. Don't hold grudges, plan paybacks, or keep bringing up old issues that once hurt your feelings. With friends—and teachers—sometimes it's better to forgive and let things go.

11. *I will stand up for what I believe.* You are becoming your own person, and you are making your own decisions about a lot of things. Make sure those decisions are based on what you believe in, not just what's popular with the people around you. You will be tempted in a million different ways in middle school, and some of those temptations will not be positive. *Stand for something or you'll fall for anything.*

12. *I will honor my parents.* They brought you up—don't let them down. Remember, if *you* mess up, it's not their fault. Grow up, suck it up, stop blaming others, and *take responsibility* (see Chapter 7).

Bottom line—you're not done growing up yet. You don't have the maturity of an adult, and that's why you aren't being treated as one yet. Unfair? That's not unfair; it's for your protection! Sometimes adults will make decisions about your life that you *strongly* disagree with. Keep in mind they are making those decisions with *your* best interests at heart. Sometimes you just have to give in and go with it.

How will you handle this? (Kids only)

o   Another student has been making fun of your religion at school.

o   You feel like you have no friends at school, and not even the teachers like you.

o   You are doing poorly in a class and the teacher will not give you extra credit.

o   Your teacher says that some assignments are posted on the Internet, and you don't have a computer.

o   You leave all your assignments in your locker, and aren't able to do your homework.

o   A teacher accuses you of cheating when you were looking around the room by accident.

o   Your best friend seems to ignore you since they met someone new.

o   Your teacher never calls you by name, and you don't think they really know who you are.

o   The most popular kids in the school want you to do something *just once* with them—something you feel is wrong.

o   You feel some of your teachers' classroom rules are unfair.

o   You are upset because you received a tardy when it really wasn't your fault.

o   You are sure one teacher simply doesn't like you.

3. Grades and Stuff: *Homework, grades, and study habits—How to assure good grades*

Here it is—one of the most important chapters in the book! Or is it? Yes, grades are important in middle school. They are the little tokens of success or failure. They are the magic keys that unlock privileges (or being grounded!). While grades are important, they are only a *part* of middle school education. There is so much more. But having said that, let's talk about what you can do to assure that your son/daughter has the greatest opportunity for successful grades in middle school.

>*Attendance.* Your child cannot succeed academically if they are not at school. Yes, there are times when your child is sick, or needs to miss school for some other reason. In such cases, the teachers will help make arrangements for missed work. But—*the student must ask.* Do not assume that teachers will always offer missed work. They won't. Having said that, no amount of make up work is as valuable as work done at school. Make sure your child comes to school and that they are absent *only* when absolutely necessary. Many lessons, illustrations, and non-textbook discussions take place in the middle school classroom. Lessons that cannot be made up. And when your child *does* have those appointments they cannot miss, try to schedule these so that your middle schooler does not miss the same class over and over. If nothing else, this is common courtesy to that teacher. A good suggestion would be to have your child choose a 'when I'm absent' buddy who can inform them of all missed work whenever they must be absent.

>*Organization.* The number one problem with nearly all middle schoolers experiencing academic difficulty is not a lack of study, or a lack of ability. *It is as lack of organization.* Organization does not come naturally to middle schoolers. *Disorganization does!* Disorganized notebooks, backpacks and lockers cause students to lose materials they need, and when study time arrives, frustration begins. Don't be afraid to come check your child's locker every once and awhile. You may find lost clothing, important papers—even borrowed jewelry! *The most important thing you*

can do to help your child succeed academically is to help them get organized. You can do this by checking for agendas, assignments, etc. on a daily basis.

Zeros. As mentioned in Chapter 1, you need to be tolerant of a low score every once and awhile, but never, never, *never* accept a 'zero' without finding out why. We all have off days, but a zero is either a careless attitude or a lesson unlearned, and both are disastrous to academic averages and character development.

Writing it down. In addition to making sure they take notes in each class, have your child keep a record of all assignments *and* completed grades. Require them to keep a folder and hang on to returned papers. More than once this will save a great deal of misunderstanding and grief, and solve the dilemma of a disputed or uncompleted assignment. Never assume your child knows how to take notes. Most don't. You may have to teach them this. *Write it down!* These should be the three most important words you teach your child when it comes to academic performance. *Check it!* Are the two most important words for *you* to remember as a diligent parent!

Never assume. Your child will come home with that first A (or F), and you'll be very proud (or not). You should be. But don't assume that *one* grade in a class is indicative of the grades they'll make the rest of the year in that class, or in all their classes. The worst thing you or your child can do is assume that one grade is an indicator of all grades to come. Understand that not only do *classes* differ, but also *tests* differ. Too, homework changes in difficulty, and the time of year—even the *weather*—can change how your child performs. Check grades on a continual basis, and don't let one or two make you either too excited or too depressed. While we're on the subject of never assuming—don't assume that just because you send notes, money, or requested information to school with your child, that the teacher automatically receives it. Your child is a middle schooler! Just as certain as they are sure they turned something in, it's sometimes as certain it never got there.

Asking questions. Encourage your child to ask questions when they don't understand. Some kids refuse to ask. They think their question will be seen as stupid, or they don't want to draw attention to themselves. But asking questions is extremely important for middle school academic success. Unfortunately, if your child waits too long to ask, and tells you they're now totally confused, it might be too late.

Preparation. One of the most effective ways to help your child succeed academically is to have them always set out the next day's books and work for school *before they go to bed.* Try this. Make it a routine. It works. Another way is to require your child to show you their agenda book and homework material from school as soon as they get home. Make this a *ticket* to whatever afternoon activity they look forward to.

Homework. Time *limits*—and time *use*—are vital in doing homework. Research has shown that ten minutes per night multiplied by the grade level is the most efficient (total) time to be allotted for homework. Even the breaks you allow them should have a time limit. Help set up a consistent, organized *schedule,* and *place* for homework to be done. If your child tells you they have no homework, require them to read. Do not break the routine or they will tell you they *never* have homework.

Homework logistics. Homework should be done at a set time, and in a set place, where it's quiet. Available should be all supplies and good lighting. The homework routine is one of the most important things you can establish to help your child succeed in middle school. Middle schoolers thrive on routine. Help establish this one. And don't forget—Homework is *independent, unmonitored practice.* It's the *kid's* homework—not yours!

Homework suggestion. Regarding homework, if your child is practicing a *skill,* ask him/her to tell you what's easy, what's hard, and how they are going to *improve.* If your child is doing a *project,* ask them what knowledge they are *applying* in the project. If they cannot answer these questions, if they are totally lost, or if they are taking forever to finish— the homework is useless. Something is wrong, and you probably need to find out what it is. Also, remember that middle schoolers generally view homework, and the skill or lesson that homework is meant to teach, as separate entities. You must help them apply the homework to real life. Whenever possible, connect homework to family activities (math to pricing items in stores, social studies to upcoming TV documentaries and family trips, language arts to films, newspaper and magazine readings, etc). This is one of the most important things you can do.

Homework limits. Homework should be considered a 'quiet time' in which you are available to help. It is best done early in the evening. If homework continues to a late hour, when bedtime comes, stay with your child until they finish at a convenient point, and put them to bed—even if that homework is not done. Sufficient sleep is second only to nutrition & nurture in the growth of teens. Their mind is only as alert as their body will allow.

How will you handle this?

o   Your child tells you they failed a quiz containing material the class was given when they were absent.

o   The teachers tell you your child's grades are low because of a lack of organization, and that they wonder if their locker might reflect this.

o   In order to help your child keep up with assignments, you ask the teachers to initial the assignment book each day. The teachers agree to do this if your child reminds them after class, and you know this isn't going to happen.

o   Your child brings home a zero, and swears they turned the assignment in.

o   Your child complains that teachers require a great deal of note taking, and they simply can't get everything written down.

o   You send money and a permission slip for a field trip to school with your child, and the teacher says he/she never received it.

4. The Choices They Will Make: *Honesty, morals, and decision-making regarding peers*

There is an expression I often tell my students: *sometimes big doors swing on small hinges.* That is, very *small* decisions can result in very *large* consequences. This is never more true than in middle school. You must emphasize to your child that wise decision-making skills—more than anything else—can make or break them in middle school. Many decisions they make there will shape the entire future of their lives.

Every year, I remind my students that important decisions they make are very much like planting a seed. They will grow only what they plant. Same kind. Nothing different. Since middle schoolers are fanatically impatient, I also remind them that the harvest of those decisions planted might not grow *quickly,* but it will grow *plenty*—much more, in fact, than the seed they planted. Middle schoolers are amazed that this rule of nature generally works in life too, and that both the good and bad 'seeds' they plant eventually grow into a great harvest. This analogy makes an impression on middle schoolers. Teach it to them.

The package they bring

As they begin middle school, your child brings with them the package of morality you have instilled in them. Matters of conscience and religion will guide them through middle school, and the values they've learned will determine the choices they make. While they may seem to stretch the parameters of those values at times, in exploring the new world that is middle school, it's usually not permanent. Don't panic when your middle schooler seems to disappoint you, or seems to have gone astray from what you taught them. If you taught them well, they'll generally return. Just be patient.

The young person they become

Middle school is the time when children become young adults. It is the time of greatest social and emotional change they will ever experience in their lives. Middle school is also the time when the choices they make, turn the package they bring, into the person they become. Whatever values you instill, as they begin middle school, teach your child that they will develop a *reputation* based upon those values, and that if they do not stand for something—it is true—they will fall for anything. Teach your child to follow their conscience in times of indecision. Teach them that, like a nail pulled from a wall, a poor choice might be *forgiven*, but the 'hole' of consequences may not be soon *forgotten*, and can remain for a long, long time. Teach them to make wise decisions and you will teach them the most important lesson they will ever learn in middle school.

The decisions they make

Lesson One here is to teach your child the difference between acting and *reacting*. I tell my students: there is a time to *bounce* (react) and a time to *absorb* (just let it go). Middle schoolers tend to live in the immediate. To them, consequences are things that are not among relevant, current issues. Teach them that in most every way, shape, and form—in middle school—*they cannot trust emotions.* Repeat: emotions—*don't trust them!* Teach your child to *think,* and never to get caught up in the mere emotional 'heat of the moment'. Wise decision-making involves understanding the difference. Help your child realize that decisions based on reacting to negative situations are seldom constructive. Acting on wise advice, careful consideration, or diligent study involves decisions that take time, and are usually correct ones. Acting—or better, *reacting* based on emotion—can result in decisions that may lead to trouble. Make sure your child knows the difference. Teach them to *think* before they act—or react—and not to let their emotions cause them to make bad decisions.

> *Decisions regarding danger.* Middle schoolers generally do not fully understand the difference between *tattling* and *alerting.* For example, they feel they will betray their own if they tattle, and often, if the consequence is of minor importance, there is no need to inform an adult. Often, kids will tell a teacher when another student is chewing gum, but the student skipping class, or arranging a fight, is 'protected'. In matters of danger, however—to themselves or to the school—even if the matter involves a

close friend—your child should understand it's important to alert adults to danger. Learning the difference between *tattling* and *alerting* can become matters of life and death. Teach them the difference.

Decisions regarding peer pressures. Your child will face peer pressure in middle school like no peer pressure they have ever faced before, or will ever face again. They may or may not discuss with you the stress of the peer pressures they're facing, but it will tempt them every day of their middle school lives. The most serious peer pressure issues will involve issues such as lying, sex, vandalism, cheating, skipping, spreading rumors, stealing, and ill-advised friendships. How you've *taught* your child about such right and wrongs will be the foundation for how they *respond* to these temptations. How you *remind* them of the importance of wise decision-making regarding these issues will determine how *successful* the decisions they make will be. Do not assume that conscience, and your foundational teachings of morality, will be enough. You will have to help them survive peer pressure throughout their middle school tenure. One way to help them is to remind them what they can do in an crucial peer pressure situation. Tell them to *blame you.* It's hard for most middle schoolers to defend personal (unpopular) decisions when the pressure becomes intense. They often give in because they feel trapped. One way out is to let them know that, as a last defense, they can avoid making a poor choice by just blaming you. "*My Mom would kill me!*" may not be the best retort to peer pressure, but it might be the one to use when there's nothing left to say.

Decisions regarding themselves. The last issue regarding wise decision-making involves personal integrity. Help your child understand that their reputation—and their name—follows them the rest of their lives, and they will have to live with many of the decisions they make. Issues of disrespect, cutting corners, poor study habits—these and more will be the entities which eventually mold your child's character in life. Teach them that they must *give* respect to *earn* respect, and how to use their brain before they engage their mouth. Every decision they will make develops a part of their future. Impress upon them the safe and effective rule of decision-making: *when in doubt, don't.* We sow an act, reap a habit, mold a character, and shape our destiny. Make sure your child understands that the things they do can develop into the person they will be, and that integrity, character, and making wise choices shape the person they will be for the rest of their lives.

Sometimes I show my students a large piece of white paper with a tiny dot on it. I ask them to focus on the paper and tell me what they see. Inevitably, they all mention the tiny dot, not the large white paper itself. I explain to them that the dot is like one very poor decision they may make. While it is certainly small compared to all the good things they may do—right or wrong—the nature of people is to focus on the dot. Teach your middle schooler to make decisions very carefully. People notice.

How will you handle this?

o   The science teacher is teaching the theory of evolution, and you and your child are worried because this conflicts with your religious belief on the subject.

o   Your child tells you that their friends are really pressuring them to do something they think might be wrong, but that all the other kids are doing it too.

o   Your child tells you that they know one of their friends is doing something inappropriate, but your child really isn't comfortable telling on them.

o   Your child tells you they got in trouble for something they didn't do just because they hang with friends who are always getting in trouble.

o   Your child tells you they don't understand why you're making a big deal about getting high grades when they are passing all their classes.

o   Your child tells you they had to lie to a teacher in order to keep a friend from getting into very serious trouble.

o   Your child tells you that you are making too big a deal about something you feel is wrong, because *"times have changed"*.

o   You discover your child is making some questionable friendships because they feel no one else really likes them.

5. All About Their Mouth: *Garbage in, garbage out—words that will make them and break them*

Middle school is all about communication. Taking notes, reading notes, passing notes, asking questions, social conversation—all these *are* middle school. As mentioned earlier, communication in middle school is vital. It affects everything from academics to relationships. Unfortunately, however, there is another manner of communication in middle school which is not only inappropriate, in most cases it is against school policy. It also makes you and your child look bad, and can sometimes result in disciplinary measures. It's called inappropriate language and gesturing.

One of the first things I do with a new class of middle schoolers is to tell them the story of *'the bucket and the well'*. It goes something like this. A middle schooler, practicing cross-country running through the fields, becomes thirsty, and stops by a well to drink. Suddenly feeling a bit ill as his breakfast starts to return on him, he 'spills' his breakfast down into the well. Later, another thirsty runner approaches the same well to draw up a bucket of the cool water. He is surprised by the previous runner's breakfast floating in the bucket. I explain to the students that the filthy water coming up from the well in the *bucket* is not the problem. The problem is the water in the *well*. The bucket is just the delivery system. After our conversation about inappropriate use of words, students quickly understand the point I am try to teach them: when filth comes out of their 'bucket', the problem lies much deeper.

Students enter middle school coming from a diverse variety of backgrounds. What is unacceptable in one family is a common occurrence in another. For example, simply saying *'shut up'* will shock one middle schooler, while another will ignore it as ordinary conversation. But for the most part, when your child enters the doors of middle school, inappropriate language and gesturing—though common—is considered totally unacceptable. Whether you teach this to your child as a part of moral or religious training, or teach it simply to keep them out of trouble in middle school, *teach it*. A middle schooler who cannot control his/her mouth is a middle schooler headed for trouble somewhere down the line. Discuss with your son/daughter the appropriateness and inappropriateness of the following methods of communication. Impress upon them the importance of being respected by school staff and administration, and how this can be affected by what comes out of their mouths.

Cursing. Everybody does it. Or at least that's what many middle schoolers think. First off, *not* everybody does it, and whether or not it's done 'at home', or 'on TV' is not the issue. Middle schoolers are expected to keep generally accepted curse words *out* of their vocabulary while at school. Do not excuse or condone inappropriate language. If you cannot discourage cursing through personal example, at least make sure you teach your child that it is not to be done at school. Remind your middle schooler that teachers are people too. Teachers form opinions about students based upon things said. Teachers are also human beings who make mistakes. Hopefully your child will never hear a teacher curse in the classroom, but that is not the issue, and not an excuse a child may use to curse. Teach your child that their teeth are not the only part of their mouth they need to keep clean.

Talking back. Middle school students have a difficult time distinguishing between *reasoning* and *arguing*. Discuss with them the importance of the difference. Middle schoolers are also notorious for *commenting*, that is, verbalizing a thought that might better be left unsaid. Stress to your middle schooler the importance of controlling comments. Teach them also that while their opinion counts, there is a time, a place, and a limit to responses they may make, and that sometimes what they *meant* may not be how it came across.

Gestures. Although a non-verbal communication, gestures and body language can be especially incendiary among middle schoolers. Make sure your child understands that gestures can often be more inflammatory than words. Middle schoolers react. And they react more strongly to an inappropriate gesture made in their direction than they might to an inappropriate comment. More than anything else, even an *unintentional* gesture interpreted incorrectly can fire up a middle schooler. Make your child understands that whether inappropriate communication is by tongue—or by finger—it is still *inappropriate* and can result in stern punishment in middle school.

Confession. Here's one that certainly seems out of place. But confession of a wrong can do more to heal a relationship with a teacher or another student than just about anything your child can say. Teach your child that when they make a mistake, the best thing to do is admit it, and not cover it with useless excuses. A well timed *'I'm sorry',* or *'I did it'* works wonders in defusing tense situations. In addition, it is something middle school teachers are *not* used to hearing, and will go a long way in developing a positive teacher/student relationship. It is not the nature of most middle schoolers to apologize or admit mistakes. But if you teach your child to do this when they are wrong—or even when they sometimes *appear* to be wrong—your child will stand out above 95% of all their peers, and earn the respect of the teachers they must work with. Teach your child that sometimes the best way to use their mouth is to *admit* their mistakes.

Compliments. Here's another magic bullet that, when used wisely and is well-timed, will greatly improve your middle schooler's chances of success with their teachers and fellow students. Middle schoolers understand *compliments* much better than they understand *confession.* Nevertheless, you will need to teach them *how* to compliment sincerely, in a timely manner, and not as an overdone 'suck up' which compliments can easily evolve into. While we're on the subject, you must understand that middle schoolers have more difficulty *taking* compliments than *giving* them. Receiving a compliment is generally an awkward moment for a middle schooler, and *'thank you'* doesn't come easy. You are probably going to have to teach your child how to graciously receive and respond to compliments. While confession may clear the air, compliments can fill it with sweet perfume.

Tone. Tone of voice does speak loudly. Sometimes it's not what your child says, but *how they say it.* Teachers are pretty adept at listening to what middle schoolers say, and if a comment feels *confrontational* to them, your child is definitely not going to win that one. For example, *"That was really interesting, Mr. Parks"* takes on quite different meanings—from praise to sarcasm—based upon the tone in which it is spoken. Emphasize to your child that quite often *how* something is said is as important as *what* is said.

Hurtful words. Teach your child never use the *'hate'* word—especially to teachers, friends, and *you.* This word leaves a hurtful and lasting scar. I tell my students that hurtful words are like arrows shot from a bow. Once they leave, you cannot know how far they'll travel, or what damage they may cause. Impress upon your child that, once spoken, they can never *unsay* hurtful words.

Misinterpretation. Middle schoolers are notorious for hearing only on the channel they happen to be thinking on. Teach your child to think before reacting to what they *thought* they heard. The message sent may have been entirely different that the message received.

Yada, yada, yada. Finally, remind your middle schooler that they don't have to say *everything!* Teach them that sometimes they can do the right thing by what they *don't* say. Some pretty damaging things have been said in the attempt at humor. Have them think it through before they comment, and if there might be a way someone could take it wrong, make sure they just don't say it. Teach them the old adage: if it can go without saying, *let it go, without saying.*

How will you handle this?

○   Your child is upset because the school made a big deal about their use of words they always use and hear at home.

○   Your child tells you they heard the teacher use inappropriate language in class.

○   Your child got in trouble for talking back to a teacher when the child says they were just trying to make their point.

○   Your child asks you why they should apologize for something they did wrong if they really don't mean it.

6. Presenting Themselves: *Impressions last, and attitude is everything!*

One of the most important lessons you can teach your child is that whether by speaking, writing, appearance, the kids they hang with—or merely by the *attitude* they bring—they present themselves in either a positive or negative way every day they come to school. Although the impressions they create in the first week or two of school are the most important, your child must understand that how they present themselves *daily* leaves a lasting impression on both adults and their peers. Help them to make *positive* impressions in middle school.

Presenting themselves through speaking. Middle schoolers love to talk but hate to speak. For the most part, in a classroom setting, they are afraid of misspeaking, answering incorrectly, or risking having the teacher—or worse, their peers—make fun of them. But one of the most important things you can teach your middle schooler is how to speak *clearly, correctly, and distinctly*. I teach my students that while good grades may lead them to the gate of success in life, the ability to speak properly is what will open the door. Whining, mumbling, and butchering the English language are not easily tolerated—by either teachers, other students, or future employers.

Presenting themselves through writing. Middle schoolers love to write notes, but hate to compose creatively as an assignment. Nevertheless, how your child learns to express his/herself through writing will determine how well they present themselves to everyone from teachers to prospective employers. They must learn to write *expressively, correctly, and appropriately*. How they write and speak will be the *first* impression they make with adults and students in middle school, and the *last* impression they'll make on a prospective employer someday if they do both poorly.

Presenting themselves through reasoning. Middle schoolers love to argue, but have great difficulty discerning between *arguing* and *discussing*. It is very important to the social (and academic) success of your child that they learn the difference. Most teachers will welcome a reasoned discussion from a student with a differing point of view. On the other hand, few if any teachers are willing to sacrifice time and authority to converse with a middle schooler who would rather argue than reason. Teach your child that *discussion* eventually concludes with either an agreeable *solution,* or an *agreement* to disagree. *Arguing* however, becomes personal, and eventually concludes in heated emotions. Arguing in middle school seldom leads to anything constructive. Your child must realize that when engaging in a classroom discussion with teachers, there will be times when they will simply have to let it go. Middle schoolers often view this as surrender, and surrendering is something middle schoolers do not do well. Teach them that sometimes it's *necessary,* not wimpy, and often a better alternative than what might happen if they don't.

Presenting themselves through appearance. Appearance is *Issue One* with middle schoolers. More than just about anything else, middle schoolers judge each other by how they look. One misconception middle schoolers have is that teachers also judge them this way. Middle school teachers are used to diversity. Students should not assume teachers won't like them if they have a different dress style. The kids might judge this way, but to a teacher, attitude is far more important. Some middle schoolers choose to dress in a manner which draws attention. This they will call 'personal expression', and as long as appearance falls within the school dress code, personal expression is fine. Your child needs to understand however, that—right or wrong—other middle schoolers will judge them by their dress style, and label them accordingly.

Presenting themselves through friendships. In middle school, other students will judge your child not only by their dress style, but also by the company they keep. Kids with a similar dress style (and interests) tend to form their own cliques, and these cliques will be labeled by other students with identifications that last a long, long time. Make sure your child understands the importance of the choosing the right friends. What their friends *are,* your child is likely to *become.* Middle school is a time of personal expression. Teach your child to make wise choices with that expression, and how to sell *themselves* without selling themselves *out.*

Presenting themselves through attitudes they bring. "*That's not fair, Mr. Parks.*" "*Don't expect life to be fair*", I tell them, "*... life isn't fair—get over it.*" Your middle schooler will probably have more issues with fairness than with any other issue. Why? Because middle schoolers are sticklers for what they see as fair, and they're not afraid to express their opinion on the subject. Often, your child will confuse *acceptability* with *fairness*. What the teacher determines as something unacceptable—in essence or in time—a middle schooler may see as unfair. Middle schoolers do not like to be compared, embarrassed, spoken to sarcastically, or generally told *no*. No teacher would intentionally mistreat a student this way, and all good teachers strive to be fair. But help your child understand that what they see as *unfair* may be something that is *unnecessary*. There are a number of other things your child may not want to hear, but you'd do well to discuss these with them. In middle school, these include:

> *Losing attitudes.* Attitude is *everything* in middle school, because attitudes usually lead to *actions,* Their attitude toward school, staff, and peers is vital in determining the social (and often academic) success or failure of your child. An attitude of wanting to fight, bullying, acting spoiled, sarcasm, being argumentative and disrespectful, etc., will immediately estrange your child from his/her peers. Not only that, it will attract to your child—as like company— those with the same characteristics. Such kids are then stereotyped, and the stereotype sticks. Another losing attitude prevalent in middle school is the selfish attitude of wanting to bring others down in order to perceive one's self as more important. Attempting to accomplish this through gossip, insults, and spreading rumors, is the typical middle schooler's *modus operendi*. Explain to your child the importance of avoiding such conduct. Spreading gossip and rumors is that one thing middle schoolers hate most in *each other* while doing most *themselves*.

> *Winning attitudes.* Winning attitudes, while less prevalent, are not lost among middle schoolers. In fact, it is the *rarity* of such attitudes which makes them most prized. Discuss with your middle schooler the importance of starting school with *positive* attitudes, such as humility, honesty, cooperation, and friendliness. Teach them to exercise a healthy sense of humor, and don't allow them to take themselves too seriously. Help them understand that, especially in

middle school, sometimes it's better to simply laugh at yourself and move on. Teach them that learning to *compromise* is often more valuable than winning, and that *sharing* is more constructive than selfishness. When things don't go their way—instead of arguing and pouting—instruct them on developing an attitude of: *"I'll rise above it—I'm better than all that"*, and life will be much easier for them—with their peers, as well as with their teachers.

Necessary attitudes. Some attitudes in middle school, your child will simply *have* to develop—whether they want to or not. Such attitudes are necessitated by the middle school environment, and are just requirements for survival. One such attitude is the attitude of *confidence.* In middle school, kids can be tough on each other. Presenting an air of self-confidence will help your child a great deal. *Never let them see you sweat* is a truism in middle school. (Remember—the confidence doesn't have to be *real*—only *perceived*). Another necessary attitude is the attitude of *acceptance.* Your child must learn to accept the things that cannot be changed in middle school, such as school rules, required homework, dress codes, lunch and hall behavior, class assignments, seating arrangements, etc. Help your child learn to *accept* things they may not like or understand, and to try to *like* things they may not want to accept. Teach them that the best is expected of the best, and if they feel they aren't getting breaks—or that they're being treated unfairly—it may not be that *less* is thought of them—but that *more* is being expected of them.

Ten Bees That Always Sting in Middle School!

1. *Back talking*—teachers hate this probably more than anything else. Sometimes saying nothing is best.

2. *Backbiting*—spreading rumors, accusing others, and feeding gossip is a bee with deadly venom.

3. *Belittling*—to make someone else feel small only shows how little a middle schooler really feels about themselves.

4. *Better than*—the attitude that says: "I'm just a little better" will ensure your middle schooler will have a life with few friends.

5. *Betraying*—blabbing a confidence entrusted by a friend is almost unforgivable in middle school. Don't make promises—or listen to secrets—you cannot keep.

6. *Blame*—always blaming others, making excuses, and not taking responsibility is a telltale sign of immaturity.

7. *Borrowing*—from kids and teachers, and never returning or paying back, is a serious *no-no*. People don't like people they can't trust.

8. *Bossy*—the attitude other middle schoolers hate most.

9. *Bratty*—that 'spoiled rotten, I deserve it, whiny attitude' is a surefire way to become unpopular.

10. *Bullying*—not only unpopular, but in most schools— illegal. This is a serious offense in today's world.

There to help. Finally, at those times when your middle schooler is having particular trouble accepting the lifestyle and changes middle school brings, remind them that there are people willing to help. Middle schoolers are especially adaptive to changes which adults sometimes have trouble dealing with. But there will be times when your child simply needs to talk over such things as school problems, personal issues, friendship crises—even issues at home—with someone who *isn't* you. A teacher, counselor, or administrator is there to meet that need. Encourage your child to take full advantage of these people when things go especially bad.

How will you handle this?

o   Your child tells you the teacher told them to stop arguing when they really were just trying to discuss an important disagreement they, and others, had with that teacher.

o   Your child asks you why it's wrong to judge people by their appearance, when, in middle school, everybody seems to.

o   Your child wants to dress in acceptable—but in your opinion, *inappropriate* clothing, and tells you it's their *'self expression'*.

o   Your child tells you they got in trouble for fighting at school, but that the other person started it.

o   Your child tells you that other kids are spreading rumors about them at school.

o   Your child complains to you that one teacher gave an assignment that was simply too long to be done in two days.

o   Your child says that the school thought a certain article of clothing they wore was inappropriate, and neither you nor your child agrees.

o   Your child says one of their classes is just too hard for them.

o   Your child brings home homework that neither they nor you have a clue on how to do.

o   Your child tells you they really will be able to do homework better if they are allowed to do it with a friend.

7. Growing Up Isn't Easy: *Responsibility. Take it*

Nobody ever said growing up was going to be easy. But there are several ways your son or daughter can show their maturity in middle school. Learning these will not only make them appear to be less of 'child', it will also help your middle schooler get along better with teachers and other students. As a parent, you certainly know what one of these is. It's called *responsibility*. Responsibility can help them get better grades, and, as we all know, even obtain a better job someday. Unfortunately, middle schoolers confuse *responsibilities* with *rights*. They need to understand that while they have the *right* to attend school, they also have the *responsibility* to behave acceptably while there. But parents, all the lectures in the world on responsibility will be totally lost on your child in middle school *if you don't hold them accountable at home!* Teach them these things well, and hold them accountable. Teachers will thank you, administrators will thank you, and—most importantly—someday, *your child will thank you too.*

Sit down with your child and impress upon them these eight things. They are tried and true for middle school success:

1. **Admit your mistakes**—Nobody is perfect, so don't act like it. Recognize when you mess up, and admit it. Learn to say, *"I'm sorry".* (See Chapter 2.) It's a stronger person who'll *admit* mistakes rather than *cover* them.

2. **Clean up your own mess**—And don't create *unnecessary* ones! At lunch, in the classroom, after activities—when you create a mess—don't expect someone else to clean up after you. Do it yourself, and put things back where you found them. Don't think vandalism is cool either. Writing on desks and walls is not cute. It's a punishable violation in middle school.

3. **Don't put things off**—Today's *delay* becomes tomorrow's *harder work.* When there are chores, homework, or other things to be done,

remember the Nike commercials: *just do it.* Start today. Get it over with!

4. **Don't make excuses**—Excuses are reasons that just don't hold water. Learn the difference between *reasons* and *excuses.* Teachers might listen to reasons. Nobody—but *nobody*—wants to hear excuses in middle school. Too many excuses, and when you *do* have a good reason no one may listen!

5. **Stop complaining**—Whining and complaining about things you don't like makes you look like a child in middle school. Sometimes there is a reason to express your opinion. But whining and complaining is never it. If you want to be treated more like an adult, act like one.

6. **Don't blame**—*You* are responsible for your actions. Take credit for the good—and the *not* so good—choices you make. Don't blame teachers, parents, or other kids for dumb moves you choose to make.

7. **Share**—Selfishness is one thing that both your peers and your teachers really won't like in middle school. If you want to fit in and make friends, share yourself, your talents, and your interests with others. Offer help when you see it might be appreciated, or maybe even when it might not be. If you keep to yourself in middle school, there are two things you can be sure of: you won't have many enemies, and you certainly won't have many friends.

8. **Your actions reflect your parents**—Right or wrong, in middle school, how you act will very often be seen as a reflection of what your parents allow at home. Think about this before you embarrass your parents as well as yourself by saying or doing something stupid. Your parents brought you up. Don't let them down.

How will you handle this?

o   Your child doesn't understand why they should pick up all of their cafeteria mess when *"that's what cafeteria workers get paid for …"*

o   Your child complains to you that there's no point in trying to be friendly at school because nobody is friendly to them.

o   Your child says that it's a free country, and they should every right to say whatever they want at school.

o   Your child says they did poorly on an assignment because they had been absent, and no one would share their notes with them.

o   You are told your child has damaged the electric pencil sharpener by sticking a pen into it. Your child says other kids have done this in the past "... *so why should I get in trouble?*"

o   Your child says that apologizing makes them look like a wimp.

8. Their Final Lesson: *The world after three o'clock—TV, school, and what the real world requires*

OK, your child is just starting middle school, so why are we talking about life after high school? Because you must help them understand there is a 'real world' out there, and the sooner they understand that, the better off they will be. Some of the things discussed here might seem a little deep for them right now, but they are important. Talk to your child about these things, and help them start off middle school on the right foot. Remember, their future begins with the habits and skills they start developing their first day in middle school!

The real world

Even though they're just beginning middle school, it's not too early to encourage your child to be thinking about what they might want to do in life. Teach them to set *goals* and *priorities*, and how to work through things in *steps*, and not through impatience. Whatever they decide—and they still have lots of time—make sure you encourage them to do what they *enjoy*. Middle schoolers tend to think of careers as being based on money alone. They have a hard time understanding that money may make them *comfortable*, but it won't necessarily make them *happy*. I tell my students how I left teaching to work in real estate earlier in my career. The money was a draw, but the money didn't satisfy. Teach your child to do what they enjoy. The concern about money should be secondary.

The real world and an extra $250,000!

Speaking of money, you might want to inform your middle schooler of what *you* already know. They'll make a whole lot more of it if they stay in school! Statistics show that if students continue their education after high school, over the course of a lifetime, they will make an extra *quarter of a million dollars* more than someone who drops out.

The real world is more than just passing middle school

This is something you'll really have to emphasize to your middle schooler. Learning doesn't just stop when they finish school. Hopefully, the things they learn in middle school will benefit them later. But the most important thing they learn in middle school is not social studies, science, math, or language arts. The most important thing they learn in middle school is learning *how* to learn. We've all heard the phrase: *'if you give a person a fish, you feed them for a day. But if you teach them how to fish, you feed them for a lifetime'.* But your child may not have heard this. Teach them how to use the Internet properly, how to research information, and where to *find* what they need to know. Teach them the importance of learning from others, not just from books and classes. Teach them how to *learn!*

The real world is tough

OK, your son or daughter may be just beginning middle school—and parents, this is tough—but they're *not* a kid anymore. It really is hard for them to understand that what they see on TV is not the real world. Problems in the real world aren't solved after the last commercial, and not everyone always lives happily ever after. Though it's obvious to you and me, you need to emphasize to your child that the world outside of school and home *isn't* going to care about them nearly as much as you—or even their teachers—do. Let them know that if they think parents and teachers are tough now, just wait till they get a boss! Explain to your child that, unlike school, life in the real world isn't divided into grading periods. Teach them that the world expects them to get things right the *first* time, and doesn't always give them second chances, extra credit, or 'make-up tests'. Make your middle schooler understand that, unlike school, the world can be *very* unforgiving. The real world, it is said, often gives the test first, and teaches the lesson later. Teach your child to take advantage of what middle school has to offer them, and to hop onboard and enjoy the ride. And while you're discussing this with them, emphasize that while they *will* make mistakes in middle school—everybody does—really *stupid* choices can be very expensive in the real world. Teach them to learn now the wise decision-making skills that will save you—and them—a lot of grief the rest of their lives!

The real world: what they really should steal!

Here's something you should encourage your middle schooler to *steal*. It's called *opportunity*. They may not think much about this now, but emphasize to them the importance of taking advantage of opportunities, and always doing their best! Some chances in life only come *once*, and fly away on speedy wings. You know this better than they do. Teach them.

Final thought

Your child will get frustrated in middle school, just as they get frustrated at home. But when middle school seems to be more than they can handle, remind them that—like living at home with you—school isn't forever. It's really just a small part of their lifetime, and they need to try to enjoy the ride and have fun. Here is a suggestion that has proved invaluable over teaching many years of middle school. Have them keep a scrapbook or memory box of their middle school years. Someday they will look back on middle school as one of the best times they ever had, and by the time high school rolls around, the opportunity to create memories so sweet will be gone forever.

How will you handle this?

- Your child gets in trouble at school for handling a situation just the way it's done on television.

- Your child wants to skip post secondary education to '*play pro ball*', and '*make real money*'.

- Your child tells you it's not all that important to do well in algebra class because they're '*not going to be using that stuff anyhow*'.

- Your child is upset because a teacher won't let them retake a failed test '*like they did in elementary school*'.

Appendix

Questions to ask when conferencing with teachers:

- ✓ Can my child attend part of this conference?
- ✓ Will there be a copy of the minutes of this conference that I can have?
- ✓ What are your planning times?
- ✓ Can we develop a plan that will help my child?
- ✓ How can I visit my child's classes?
- ✓ How can my child make a phone call?
- ✓ Is my child being challenged?
- ✓ Is my child making friends?
- ✓ Is my child making *appropriate* friends?
- ✓ Is my child paying attention in class?
- ✓ Is there a syllabus that will show me what my child is going to learn this year?
- ✓ Can I get back into school after hours?
- ✓ Until what time can my child get into his/her locker after school?
- ✓ What are class policies for late work and deadlines?
- ✓ What are the class policies for makeup work?
- ✓ What is the policy on cell phones?
- ✓ What will happen if my child is sick or injured?
- ✓ My child has an inhaler, what's the policy on it?
- ✓ Is there a school nurse?
- ✓ How can I send ibuprofen or other OTC medicines to school with my child?
- ✓ What's the dress code?
- ✓ How can I contact the administration or teachers?
- ✓ Will there be a need or reason for my child to have money at school?
- ✓ Are there ever opportunities for my child to buy snacks or drinks?
- ✓ How will I know when those are?
- ✓ When do grades get sent home?

Some guidelines for parent-teacher communication:

o   Don't call teachers at home.

o   Don't call teachers during class.

o   Don't talk about your child's performance at open houses.

o   Don't ask teachers to talk about other children.

o   Come with the attitude that these teachers want to help.

o   Don't schedule a conference that will have to be rushed though.

o   Try to start off and end on a positive note.

o   Bring any documentation you are wanting to discuss (test papers, etc.).

o   If you aren't understanding what they're talking about—stop them and make them make it clear.

o   Present yourself as an ally—not a foe. Remember—you and the teachers are a team. Neither side should boss the other side around.

o   If you want to know your child's grades, *ask*. Don't expect the teacher to call you when there's a minor issue. Teachers have 150 students to deal with. You don't.

o   If your child's teacher is describing misbehavior, remember kids act differently at home and at school.

o   Keep in mind, the teacher really does want the best for your child, too! If they bring up an issue that is uncomfortable, they must really believe it's a possible problem.

o   Keep all the papers you are given—you may want to look back through them.

o   If you have talked with the teachers, and still aren't happy with the results of the conference, call the school administration and ask for a conference with them.

o   Ask for your child to attend the last part of the conference so they can see you and the teachers as a united front, and can understand the plan, also.

o   Focus on solutions rather than emphasizing the problem.

o   Schedule a future conference if necessary. Arrange for some type of follow-up.

o   Deal in specifics. Do not waste your time, or the teachers', in vague generalities.

o   Focus on strengths as well as weaknesses. Every child has both.

Addressing the Multiple Intelligences

Every child learns in different ways. These learning styles are called multiple intelligences. Understanding the strengths of your child's learning styles will enable both you and them to achieve greater success in middle school. To get some insight as to how your child learns best, sit down with them and have them take the following test, courtesy of Nancy Faris. It is unscientific, but a good indicator of learning styles. Have your middle schooler simply answer *yes* or *no* to each question. When they finish, go to the scoring rubric that follows. Afterward, you might look at the characteristics of each learning style, as well as descriptors and possible career avenues. Remember, your middle schooler may show strength though more than one learning style, and learning styles may vary over time.

How do I learn best?

1.   I am good at copying what people say.
2.   I really love books.
3.   I really like to listen to the radio.
4.   I really like to do "word searches" or crossword puzzles.
5.   I really like language arts and social studies in school.
6.   I really like to do experiments.
7.   I really like math.
8.   I really like science.
9.   I am good at making and figuring out patterns.
10. I often wonder about how things work.
11. I really like music.
12. People tell me that I sing well.
13. I know many songs by heart.
14. I sing songs I've heard on TV to myself as I'm going somewhere.
15. I would be very sad if there was no music in the world.
16. I am good at doing puzzles.
17. I am good at reading maps.
18. I hardly ever get lost or mixed up where I am going.
19. I can pretend I am in the sky looking down on my house and know where everything is.
20. I am good at drawing or making things with clay.
21. I am good at sports.
22. I really like to dance.

23. I like to be outside a lot.
24. I am good at learning new sports or dances.
25. I can figure out how something works or how to fix something that's broken by myself.
26. I feel sad when others are feeling sad.
27. I feel happy when I am with others that are feeling happy.
28. I like playing games with a group of people better than just one other person.
29. I have more than three good friends.
30. I really like being in the middle of a crowd.
31. I really like to spend time alone to think by myself.
32. I think a lot about the future and what I want to do when I grow up.
33. I know right away when I am feeling "stressed out" and I spend time alone to feel better.
34. I know right away when I am feeling "stressed out" and I spend time alone to feel better.
35. Most of the time I'd rather stay home than go out somewhere with a lot of people.
36. I enjoy camping trips a lot.
37. I would enjoy teaching others how to make a fire.
38. I love to study insect species, and plant varieties.
39. I would rather spend the night in a tent than my own bed.
40. I enjoy visiting going on trips, and visiting other places.

Scoring the results

There are no right or wrong answers. The questions are grouped according to type of learning style. If your child replied *yes* to more than 3 questions in any of these groups, these are the areas of learning in which they are the strongest.

1-5   Linguistic/Verbal
6-10   Logical/Mathematical
11-15   Musical/Rhythmic
16-20   Spatial/Visual
21-25   Bodily/Kinesthetic
26-30   Interpersonal
31-35   Intrapersonal
36-40   Naturalistic

Learning styles

Linguistic/Verbal (Attorneys, Authors, Ministers, Sales!)
"Just give me the words, man—I think in words!"

Involves creative reading, writing, and storytelling
Encourage your middle schooler to share ideas
Encourage your middle schooler to debate an issue
Encourage your middle schooler to create a presentation
Work with your middle schooler on vocabulary terms
Encourage your middle schooler to study etymology
Encourage your middle schooler to study using flash cards, word associations, and *Jeopardy*-type games
Teach your middle schooler through puns, similes, metaphors, and limericks

Logical/Mathematical (Accountants, Scientists, Computer programmers, Detectives!) *"I'm think in the abstract, and I'm a problem-solver!"*

Encourage your middle schooler to perform experiments
Encourage your middle schooler to design a graph or timeline
Encourage your middle schooler to utilize prediction, solve a dilemma or evaluate an idea, decision, video, or book
Encourage your middle schooler to utilize *compare* and *contrast*
Encourage your middle schooler to create a code or symbol activity, and use syllogisms, analogies, etc.
Encourage your middle schooler to interpret data, utilize prediction of consequences, or design a puzzle

Musical/Rhythmic (Musicians, composers!)
"If I can hear it, I can ..."

Encourage your middle schooler to sing songs, or write a jingle
Encourage your middle schooler to research a musician
Encourage your middle schooler to analyze a commercial
Allow your child to play background music during homework times

Spatial/Visual (Artists, Interior decorators, Architects, Photographers!)
"If I can see it, I can ..."

> Encourage your middle schooler to make a collage, create a brochure, or design a poster
> Emphasize color and perspective in your child's world
> Use pictures and photos to teach your child
> Show videos, documentaries, or educational films
> Encourage your middle schooler to utilize their imagination, illustrate a story, or utilize diagramming and visualization scenarios

Bodily/Kinesthetic (Athletes, Surgeons, Dancers, Carpenters!)
"Let's get down and DO it, baby!"

> With your middle schooler, play a charade or pantomime game
> Encourage your middle schooler to debate an issue
> Encourage your middle schooler to join in athletic activities
> Encourage your middle schooler to perform in a play, or role-play an event
> Relate learning to sports whenever possible, take them on trips, and work with manipulatives

Interpersonal (Politicians, Teachers, Actors!)
"Let's do it together!"

> Encourage your middle schooler to participate in group presentations, or role-play!
> Allow your child to work on problem-solving activities
> Utilize E-mail and telephone activities
> Encourage your middle schooler to debate an issue

Intrapersonal (Theologians, Philosophers, Psychologists!)
"Can I just think about this awhile?"

> Encourage your middle schooler to keep a journal
> Allow your child a time of sustained silent reading
> Encourage them at home to reflect and write about issues and events
> Encourage your middle schooler to do self-study quizzes and inventories

Naturalistic (Ecologists, Zoologists!)
"If we can GO, I'll GROW!"

> Encourage your middle schooler to get involved outdoor activities, go on hikes and camping trips, and utilize pictures with photos
> Have your child do nature studies

Character counts

Personal character is a big part of the life your middle schooler will live as they begin the 6th grade. Listed are the generally accepted tenets of character development that make up various character education programs. Go over each tenet, and have your middle schooler:

✓   Tell you what they think each means.

✓   Look up and define the accepted definition of what each means.

✓   Discuss with you a situation *when* and *why* each of these might be used.

✓   Tell you right and wrong choices which could be made, and *why*.

Altruism
Citizenship
Courtesy
Honesty
Human worth
Justice
Knowledge
Respect
Responsibility
Self-discipline

My personal philosophy of life inventory

Here's a little survey you might have fun doing with your child. Have them think about and complete the following statements. Discourage one word, or senseless answers. They may not answer a question with the opposite, for example, they may not say: An apple is: '*not a pear*'. Be prepared though. You may find out some interesting things about your middle schooler of which you were not aware!

1. Truth is:

2. Knowledge is:

3. Power is:

4. Rules are:

5. It's important to know:

6. I would like to tell my friends:

7. I would like to tell my family:

8. I would like to tell my teachers:

9. I'm happy when:

10. A goal in life I have is:

11. The best thing about my age is:

12. Another age I'd like to be is:

13. The last thing that made me feel really bad was:

14. The most important person I've ever known was:

15. The most important person ever born was:

16. I really feel good when:

17. When I need to feel better, I:

18. A friend is:

19. The best thing about my gender is:

20. The worst thing about my gender is:

21. When I think of the future:

22. I worry most about:

23. A good teacher:

24. If I had a role model, it would be:

25. The best thing about school is:

26. The worst thing about school is:

27. A good student:

28. Grades are:

29. God is:

30. Someday, I'd like to be a:

Helpful websites

Here are some helpful and entertaining websites which were current as of the publishing of this book:

http://www.journalistexpress.com/
http://www.scholastic.com/schoolage/middleschool/homework/index.htm
http://www.geocities.com/Athens/Academy/6617/
http://www.refdesk.com/
http://www.factmonster.com/world.html
http://www.homeworkspot.com/
http://encarta.msn.com/encnet/departments/homework/
http://www.braingle.com/
http://quizhub.com/quiz/quizhub.cfm
http://www.schoolnotes.com/
http://www.top100familysites.com/index.shtml
http://www.refdesk.com/homework.html#jrhi
http://dictionary.reference.com/
http://www.fun-with-words.com/index.html
http://www.infoplease.com/

About the Author

Jerry Parks earned his B.S., M.A., & Ed.S degrees in Education from Eastern Kentucky University, and completed additional graduate work at the University of Kentucky. He is a *Nationally Board Certified Teacher*, has received numerous "Teacher of the Year" honors at the local, state, and national level, and is a member of the 2007 USA TODAY *All American Teacher Team*. He is a regular speaker at the *National Middle School Association*, and *National Council for the Social Studies* conferences, and is currently instructor of 7th grade social studies at Georgetown Middle School in Georgetown, Kentucky.

Dr. Parks has several previously published books, including:

"Teacher Under Construction", a survival handbook for new middle school teachers.

"So, You Want to Become a National Board Certified Teacher?", a handbook for teachers considering the National Board Certification process.

"Mentoring the NBPTS Candidate", a handbook for mentors of the National Board Certification process.

"With Joseph in the University of Adversity: The Mizraim Principles", a study of the life of the Old Testament hero, Joseph.

"God, Help Me Pray!", and *"God, Help Me Pray!: Workbook and Journal"*, teachings on prayer from a Biblical perspective.

"Dragons, Grasshoppers, & Frogs!", a handbook for teenagers and new Christians on the Book of Revelation.

Dr. Parks can be reached via e-mail at:
kidztchr7@hotmail.com

978-0-595-46529-3
0-595-46529-3

CPSIA information can be obtained at www.ICGtesting.com
Printed in the USA
LVOW091707240412

278949LV00006B/103/A